Rookie

Re J 696.182 Mat
Mattern, Joanne
Sc Toilets

WITHDRAWN

$5.95
ocn909112374

How Things Work:

Toilets

D1104033

by Joanne Mattern

Content Consultant
Nanci R. Vargus, Ed.D.
Professor Emeritus, University of Indianapolis

Reading Consultant
Jeanne M. Clidas, Ph.D.
Reading Specialist

Children's Press®
An Imprint of Scholastic Inc.

A CIP catalog record of this book is available from the Library of Congress.
ISBN 978-0-531-21372-8 (library binding) – ISBN 978-0-531-21460-2 (pbk.)

No part of this publication may be reproduced in whole or in part, or stored in a retrieval system, or transmitted in any form or by any means, electronic, mechanical, photocopying, recording, or otherwise, without written permission of the publisher. For information regarding permission, write to Scholastic Inc., Attention: Permissions Department, 557 Broadway, New York, NY 10012.

Produced by Spooky Cheetah Press
Design by Keith Plechaty

© 2016 by Scholastic Inc.

All rights reserved. Published in 2016 by Children's Press, an imprint of Scholastic Inc.

Printed in China 62

SCHOLASTIC, CHILDREN'S PRESS, ROOKIE READ-ABOUT®, and associated logos are trademarks and/or registered trademarks of Scholastic Inc.

1 2 3 4 5 6 7 8 9 10 R 25 24 23 22 21 20 19 18 17 16

Photographs ©: cover: Mike Clarke/AFP/Getty Images; 3 top left: rasslava/iStockphoto; 3 top right: Sasha Radosavljevic/iStockphoto; 3 bottom: Manit321/iStockphoto; 4: baobao ou/Getty Images; 7: photopixel/Shutterstock, Inc.; 11: Ryan McVay/Thinkstock; 15: NarisaFotoSS/Shutterstock, Inc.; 16: llucky78/iStockphoto; 19: AuntSpray/Shutterstock, Inc.; 21 main: Mary Evans Picture Library/Alamy Images; 21 inset: Miguel Sobreira/age fotostock/Superstock, Inc.; 22: Kumar Sriskandan/Alamy Images; 25: Zuma Press, Inc./Alamy Images; 26 background, 27 background: phokin/Shutterstock, Inc.; 26, 27 roll of toilet paper: albund/Shutterstock, Inc.; 26 left: Mary Evans Picture Library/Alamy Images; 26 right: Kumar Sriskandan/Alamy Images; 27 left: irina88w/Thinkstock; 27 right: Zuma Press, Inc./Alamy Images; 30: NASA/Reuters; 31 top: Miguel Sobreira/age fotostock/Superstock, Inc.; 31 center: Ryan McVay/Thinkstock; 31 bottom: NarisaFotoSS/Shutterstock, Inc.

Illustrations by Jeffrey Chandler/Art Gecko Studios!

Table of Contents

Down the Drain

Have you ever thought about how a toilet works? What really happens when you flush?

Toilets can be fancy or plain. But most of them have two main parts. The tank is the top part. You sit on the bowl. Both the tank and the bowl are full of water.

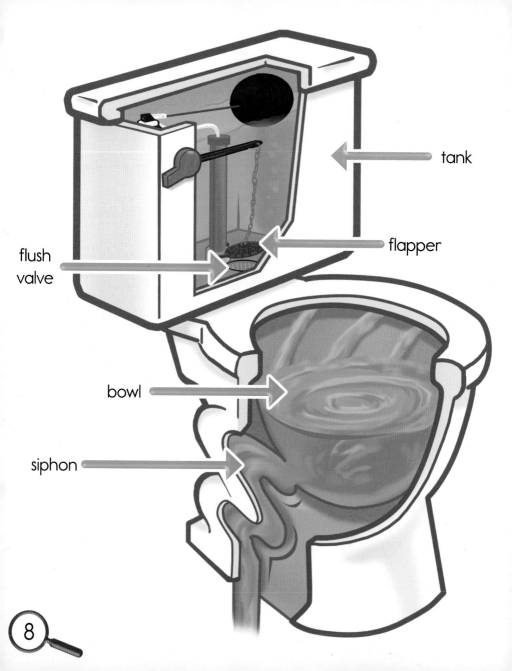

tank

flapper

flush
valve

bowl

siphon

8

When you **flush**, a chain pulls up a flapper in the tank. *Whoosh!* The water goes down a hole called the flush valve.

Now water rushes into the bowl.
It flows down the hole into a tube
called the **siphon**. Water and waste
are sucked through the siphon.

About two gallons of water rushes
into the bowl every time you flush.

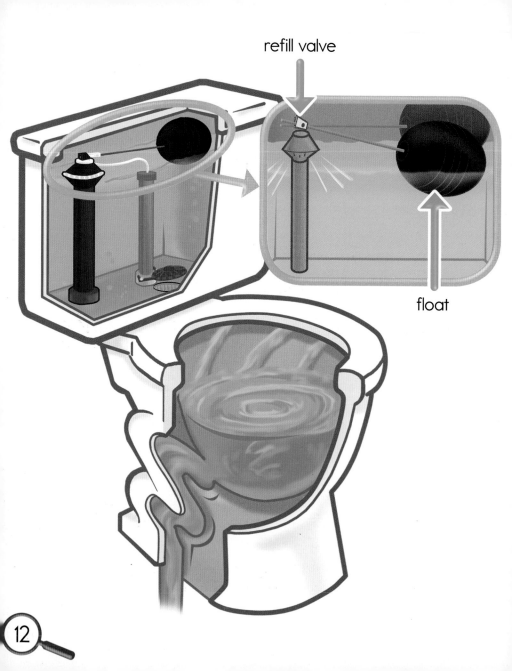

refill valve

float

How does the toilet fill back up? As the water level falls in the tank, so does the float. It pulls the refill valve open and water pours in. The tank fills and the float moves up again. That turns off the water.

FUN FACT!

Airplane toilets are not filled with water. Air sucks the waste into a hole. Then it goes into a big tank. Once the plane lands, a worker vacuums out the tank.

Where Does It Go?

When you flush the toilet, the waste does not stay in your house. Every toilet is connected to a larger system. A pipe carries the waste out of the house.

A plumber installs pipes under a house. They carry away waste from the toilet.

Some toilets are connected to a **sewer** system. A pipe connects each building to a bigger pipe under the street. That pipe carries waste to a treatment plant. The wastewater is cleaned.

A worker tests the water at a treatment plant.

Some houses have a septic system. A pipe carries waste to a big tank under the ground. The waste gets broken down in the tank. The water drains out into the yard. Everything else stays in the tank.

FUN FACT!

A septic tank must be pumped out every one to three years.

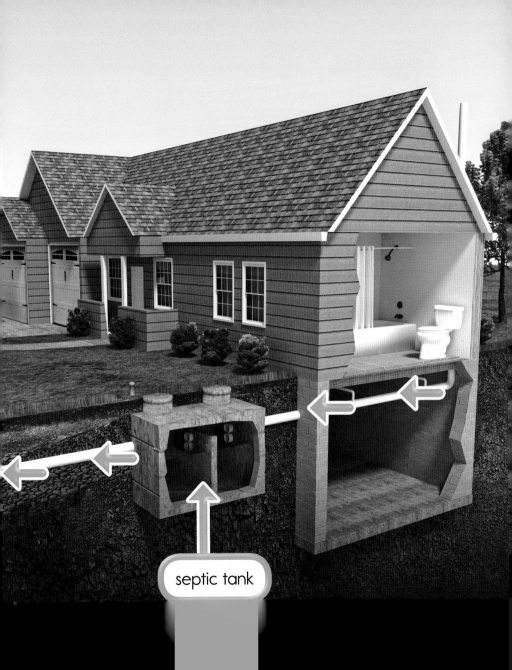

septic tank

Before the Toilet

People have always had to get rid of their waste. The ancient Romans had a sewer system. Later, some castles even had toilets. But these were more like indoor outhouses than modern toilets.

A lot of people went to the bathroom in **chamber pots**. Then they dumped the chamber pots out the window!

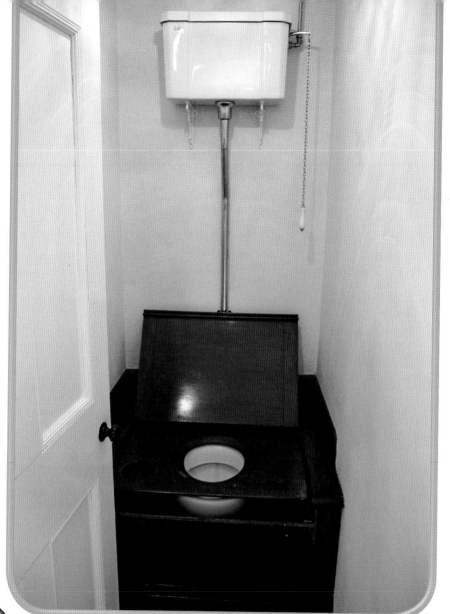

The flush toilet was invented in 1596. The tank was on the ceiling. Pulling a chain on the tank released water into the bowl. Still, most people continued to use a chamber pot.

Almost 200 years later, Alexander Cummings made a better toilet. He created the S-shaped pipe under the bowl. This kept bad smells from coming up through the pipes.

Building a Better Toilet

Toilets can use a lot of water. That can be wasteful. Some newer toilets use fewer gallons for each flush. A dual-flush toilet has one button for a small flush and another button for a big flush.

Now you know how toilets work. These simple machines get a dirty job done right!

small flush

big flush

flusher on a
dual-flush toilet

500–1500s
People use chamber pots.

1596
Sir John Harington invents the flush toilet.

mid-1900s

Indoor toilets become popular in the United States.

1993

Dual-flush toilets become available.

Super Science

Ask an adult for help. Do not attempt this science experiment on your own!

The siphon is an important part of what makes a toilet flush. This experiment shows how it works.

You Will Need: Toilet, several cups of water, bucket of water (about 2 gallons)

1.

Pour a cup of water into the toilet. You will see that nothing happens.

2. Pour more cups of water into the toilet. Again, nothing happens. That is because the extra water spills over the edge of the siphon and runs down the drain.

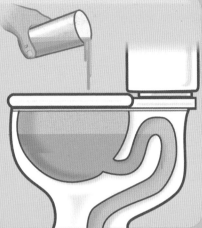

3. Now pour the bucket of water into the toilet. The toilet flushes!

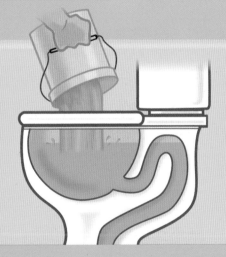

Why This Works:

You poured enough water into the toilet to fill the siphon. The filled siphon sucked the water out of the bowl and down the drain.

That's Amazing!

Ever wonder how astronauts use the toilet in space? For one thing, they have to fasten themselves to the toilet to keep from floating away!

A space toilet uses a rush of air instead of water to flush waste away. Then a vacuum sucks up the waste. Liquid waste is sent out into space. Solid waste is dried and stored in a special bag that is brought back to Earth.

The toilet on the International Space Station cleans the wastewater so astronauts can drink it.

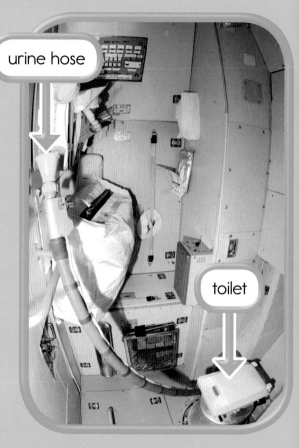

urine hose

toilet

Glossary

chamber pots (CHAYM-bur POTS): small pots used as toilets

flush (FLUHSH): wash away waste with moving water

sewer (SOO-er): series of pipes that carry away waste

siphon (SYE-fuhn): tube that sucks away liquids

Harris County Public Library
Houston, Texas

Index

Facts for Now

Visit this Scholastic Web site for more information on toilets:
www.factsfornow.scholastic.com
Enter the keyword **Toilets**

About the Author

Joanne Mattern is the author of many nonfiction books for children. Science is one of her favorite subjects to write about! She lives in New York State with her husband, four children, and numerous pets.